This book belongs to

_____

This book is dedicated to my children - Mikey, Kobe, and Jojo.

By Mary Nhin

Illustrated By
Yuliia Zolotova

Kobe Bryant

Hi, I'm Kobe Bryant.

BLACK MAMBA

I always knew I was going to play professional basketball. My dad was an NBA player, and he started teaching me to play when I was three.

When we moved to Italy, I was worried I'd lose my chance to play. It was a challenge not being able to watch my favorite NBA players. I didn't want to miss out, so my grandfather mailed me tapes of all the NBA games and wrote to me to keep me up to date.

It was hard work for me, because I had to learn a new language and start at a new school. But I made the time to study the tapes and I learned how to speak Italian.

I was determined to make the most of everything I had, watching the players and imitating them in my own games. I might have missed out on the American culture growing up, but I would master the sport.

I played summer league basketball in the U.S. every year. Eventually, I moved back to America to go to high school.

My years of practice paid off. I made it onto the basketball varsity team as a freshman and won awards for MVP and Player of the Year. I was good enough to win a college scholarship.

My ultimate goal was joining the NBA, though.
I couldn't wait, so at the age of 17, I made
the decision to go directly into the NBA.

Thanks to my determination, I signed with the Los Angeles Lakers. I was the first NBA guard to be signed straight out of high school, but I more than proved I was ready for it.

In 1997, during a must-win playoff game, I had the ball in my hands in the final moments against the Utah Jazz. I shot with confidence, but on this night, instead of game-winning glory, I got four air balls and we lost in overtime.

It was a turning point for me. I spent the entire offseason working on my shots until the sun came up.

Many people quit after massive defeat,
but I refused to give up.

I would go on to have 36 game-winning shots in my career. I would win five NBA Championships and be named NBA All-Star eighteen times before I retired.

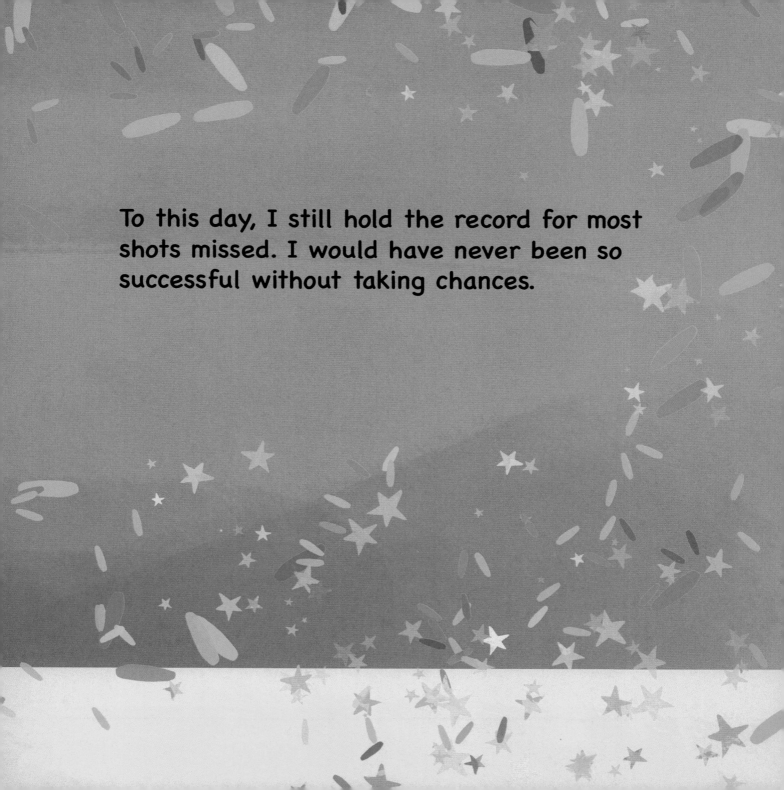

To this day, I still hold the record for most shots missed. I would have never been so successful without taking chances.

I have self-doubt. I have insecurity. I have fear of failure. I have nights when I show up at the arena and I'm like, 'My back hurts, my feet hurt, my knees hurt. I don't have it. I just want to chill.' We all have self-doubt. You don't deny it, but you also don't capitulate to it. You embrace it.

Timeline

1997 – Kobe becomes the youngest Slam Dunk
      Champion in history

2000 — Kobe and the Lakers win first NBA
      championship together

2001 — Kobe and the Lakers win second NBA
      championship together

2002 — Kobe and the Lakers perform a three peat

2008 – Kobe is named NBA Most Valuable Player and
      plays on the team that wins Gold at the Olympics

2010 – Kobe becomes NBA champion for the fifth
      time in his career

2012 – Kobe wins gold at the Olympics again

2021 - Kobe still holds record for most shots
      missed – 14,481 missed shots

minimovers.tv

 @marynhin   @GrowGrit
#minimoversandshakers

 Mary Nhin   Ninja Life Hacks

 Ninja Life Hacks

 @marynhin

Made in the USA
Middletown, DE
07 January 2022

58118312R00020